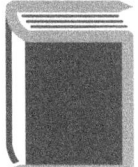

THE HAUNTED HOUSE

Marisa Crawford

SWITCHBACK BOOKS

CHICAGO

Copyright © 2010 Marisa Crawford. All rights reserved.
No part of this book may be reproduced
without the permission of the publisher.

ISBN-13: 978-0-9786172-5-7
ISBN-10: 0-9786172-4-X

Library of Congress Control Number: 2009934156

Book design: Erika Snell.

Cover art: Orion Shepherd.

Switchback Books
Brandi Homan, *Editor-in-Chief*
Becca Klaver and Hanna Andrews, *Founding Editors*
Daniela Olszewska, *Assistant Editor*
PO Box 478868
Chicago, IL 60647
editors@switchbackbooks.com
www.switchbackbooks.com

ACKNOWLEDGMENTS

Grateful acknowledgment goes to the editors of the following publications, in which versions of these poems first appeared:

Big Bell: "The River," "Swan Song," "Swimming in Lanes Five and Six"; *GlitterPony*: "Me Without Makeup"; *Invisible Ear*: "Perfect Blue Orbs," "For Cera," "Indian Summer"; *Parthenon West Review*: "California"; *Poetry Flash*: "The Cute Beatle"; *Shampoo*: "Valentine's Day."

Thanks to Switchback Books editors Brandi Homan, Hanna Andrews, and Becca Klaver for their hard work and dedication to supporting and publishing women poets, and to Denise Duhamel for selecting *The Haunted House* for publication. A special thank you to Orion Shepherd for creating beautiful artwork for the book cover.

Many thanks to the following for the support, encouragement, and inspiration that made this book possible: Seth Landman, Dave Iwaszkiewicz, Matt Rohrer, Chrissy Anderson-Zavala, Jason Morris, the Girlshop girls, and my teachers at the San Francisco State University MFA Program, especially Toni Mirosevich and Truong Tran. Special thanks to my family for their support and love.

For all the girls, real and make-believe

TABLE OF CONTENTS

Ghost Story 15
The Bible Belt 16
The River 17
Field Notes 18
Deidre 19
Perfect Blue Orbs 20
The Center 21
Barging Into 22
Pachyderm 23
Chick Flicks 24
Ivy, The Name of this Poem is Secret 25
For Cera 26
And I Will Always Love You 27
Valentine's Day 28
The Cute Beatle 29
For Cera 30
California 31
What Happened in the Pool 32
The Haunted House 35
Tidal 47
Indian Summer 48
Swimming in Lanes Five and Six 49
Swan Song 50
Under the Evergreens 51
A Letter 52
This Summer 54
For Cera 55
Yellow jackets 56
From the Place Where All the Postcards Come 57
I Drew a Door 58
For Cera 59
Water 60
Me Without Makeup 61
Book Eater 62
Yum Poison Apple 63
For Cera 64
Skull & Crossbones 65

The Logician 66
Briar Rose 67
Riding in Cars with Monsters... 68
Called Back 69
I Had Never Felt So Much Like a Cake Made up
    of a Variety of Ingredients.. 70
Artifacts.. 71

Ghost Story

I saw Bigfoot there,
a cherry red heart
formation in the middle
of the pond. Thought maybe
the twitch in my eye could be
you tugging at my eyeliner,
all the black birds lined up
on a telephone wire. Hello?
I'd like to thank the seeds,
all the seeds that turned into trees
after everyone said they'd never grow.
Thank the part of the movie
where the girl says, *Hold me.* I was
wearing earmuffs the size of full moons
and the road was filling up with snow.

The Bible Belt

There is a book about a girl who knew everything was wrong because of her red hair. And a book written as if the writer was a girl who lived in a box with only a typewriter. And there are various testing methods for qualifying best friends, methods that involve wind and windbreakers and how well your arms wrap around pillows and how tight your hands grip the monkey bars and how sweet is your singing voice.

Stephanie belted songs like a siren, soaked the whole house in honey, left her own slumber party to ride her bike in the driveway, and I woke up, could have sworn she was screaming but it was just the cotton flowers on her undershirt. I could have sworn it was blood but it was just her hair. And what would you steal and not steal from the school store and what would you bury and not bury?

How many times have we fought? Does your house have secret passageways? Do you swear to God with uncrossed fingers? Prove it. If your neighbor was an old man and he gave you ice cream and jewelry and you saw two hundred dollars lying on his kitchen counter, would you take it? What if Stephanie told you that Somalia was the name of her hair color, and these are shards of haunted crystal that she found in a lagoon in Cancun and she came from a far-off place filled with peaches and churches and peach ice cream and her mother died when she was born.

And this bruise is from a mustached man in a van and that she escaped, that she talked on the phone for two whole hours to the boy with the suicide pact and the cigarettes and she let him put his hand under her bra and she wears a bra and it was right past the field, right near the driveway to the school.

Stephanie's eyes were two big fat bluebirds and she flew so high on the swing set. She had a book filled with all the world records. And a book that says God forgives everyone. What if she told you that God forgives everyone? She's just like me in every way but the lacy things she wears under her clothes, top-secret sequins that cinch her waist and Jesus saves. He's like Stephanie, all the places she goes when school gets out. She rides in the back of his pickup throwing scented markers and drawing paper to kidnapped children. She wipes the makeup off runaways with warm water.

The River

Jessie baked me Funfetti birthday cupcakes in wafer cones to show all you can do with twenty-four hours when you're happy. My mother always lined a sweater box with foil, packed the cupcakes in. Storms slam the trees and power lines and we light candles during blackouts. I keep a phone with a cord and a butterfly hologram sticker in my room. And I call Jessie to talk about going to the woods behind the school where there's a pretend river. You hold hands and tiptoe stones to cross it. It's okay to be scared of slipping as long as you laugh hard. Jessie told her boyfriend *I love you* on the tire swing at the playground. The boy with the cinnamon gum and dog tags took me into the stacks at study hall to look at the caveman book. When I got to the party he had saved me a Corona in his jacket. Jessie's been engaged four times since the 8th grade and we're both hypoglycemic which means we eat sour apple fast-acting glucose squares on the steps where they take school pictures and that is all we eat. It doesn't work when we suck the air out of balloons, or out of the whipped cream can. The lady in the movie threw her sweet blue heart in the ocean and we cried for three whole days. Jessie's sister got thrown out of a car by her boyfriend but it's okay because she hits him too, and we talk all night about how we were both born in June and pluck our eyebrows when we're angry and can't ever stop talking. And we drain entire jars of icing and lick the tin foil, roll laughing with cords twirled around our fingers every time the candles knock out and sparkle back to life again.

Field Notes

Three-legged race with boy and girl.
Three-legged race with girl and girl.
The Garbage Pail Kid where one half is a girl and one half is a boy, that I never gave to Angela but always meant to.

Cookie cutter in the shape of a pine tree/ there has to be one.
Cookie cutter in the shape of a palm tree. Where are we?
Tell me there are baby monkeys on the island.

I have asthma, so I couldn't really run around the field. So I had to walk. I have allergies. I couldn't really run around the field but I was always really cool about it.

Pine tree–shaped stencil applied to denim so the outline of the tree is like this bleedy neon green, remember that? What's grosser than gross? Those spit bugs that you find sometimes on the trees, on places where the pine needle meets bark, and it looks like a little wad of spit, like somebody spit in the tree, and I thought someone did, until I poked at the spit wad with a twig and there was a bug inside. And sometimes people kiss under those trees.

That weird winter when we were obsessed with keeping caterpillars as pets. And they froze. We thought maybe the ice was a chrysalis.

The summer when there were tons of little grasshoppers the color of pebbles back in the part of the field that was covered in pebbles.

Deidre

Someone said Schenevus and Deidre said, *Bless you*, I'll give you the Claddagh ring if you promise you'll wear it forever. Heart points at the heart. Oh, heaven. If heaven had a name, if heaven sent a January angel, it would be called Deidre. If girls woke up in fawn spots, wrapped in blankets, it would be called Deidre. If the pancake batter smoothed to silk, she would be called. Deidre. Breakfast is ready when you are.

Deidre said barn red paint from the playhouse got all over her shorts and panties. Monopoly. It's perfectly quiet 'til she blares the stereo at bedtime. And plastic cherry perfume pours up the eaves and out the windows. *Pop goes Perfection*. If heaven was a cousin, if heaven was a two-piece for the swimming pool, song about spinning with the stars above. They say in heaven, houses have their stories. And you can push thumbtacks into the walls. You can kiss all the posters goodnight. And if you win the coin toss, you get to share her bed, her electric blanket and Pillow Person with upstairs windows for eyes. If heaven was a girl, she'd go up in waves. She would have to grow.

She'd get a ring on her finger, heart turned to the heart, bread baking in the oven. A house hung with wind chimes and shingles and babies tucked into their beds. If heaven was a house, what bone structure. What windows to leap from when it all starts burning. Deidre rolls out of bed and crawls to the door. Grabs the babies instead of the baby pictures. Her arms cushion the fall. Her voice cradles.

Deidre said she'd curl my bangs with the curling iron if I promised I would leave them. There is no ring on my finger. Lost it somewhere. Hairsprayed for Friday night roller-skating, we'd hike up our scrunch socks. Sneak down the drainpipe. And when the lights stopped and the music changed, we'd squeal through our hair. Deidre said, *Hold my hand*. The DJ says it's time to go backward.

Perfect Blue Orbs

Virginia draws swirling mushrooms and classic rock quotes all over her notebook. Her mother rubs graves on weekends, wears big silver rings and fishnet shirts and knows all about the real ghosts in our town. The white lady who slips under car tires and the raggedy dolls in glass cases. The girl whose Ouija board kept coming back and the men who leave handprints all over your blankets.

She says just pray to God. Just have faith in God when the little girl gets pinned to her bed by invisible hands. Faith in God past the shadow of her sapphire necklace on the wall. Just faith in God's love almighty rock garden and driveway where we braid flowers, burn pictures, and sing along.

Virginia and I trace our names in the living room carpet. Rainy days. She tells me to sleep with healing stones underneath my pillow. Virginia's mother's on the kitchen counter, handing out menthol cigarettes, assigning moon signs, blowing smoke at the ceiling. Mutable air. She says follow your heart, sweetie, says it will lead you on the path. That everything happens for a reason and of all the things I've lost I miss—Virginia and you are two lost souls swimming. When your life flashes, when there's only one set of footprints, hand me my moonstone, my amethyst, my lighter, the telephone, sweetheart. When the wind's tapping and you're looking for faces in the overexposures, that's 'cause God was carrying you.

The Center

In our book, two sisters drew a chalk line down the center of their tree house, their faces bleeding across the page gutter, saying wherever she is, she has the same room as me, does something or another that makes her happy, keeps piles of laundry and the TV on police shows where girls get killed nonstop and the neighbors don't think it's a coincidence that the paint on her walls is called *champagne*, that at the cousin's high school graduation we sat in bleachers and the valedictorian asked what we should do now, if we should just sit around and not do anything 'cause we're too scared, and her pinky was halfway linked with mine, faces are shaped like the track around the football field and she was the only one who cheered.

Barging Into

I developed early. An explosion in the school cafeteria, sprinkler system turning all the trays into little ships. This family is a fountain, four women and thirsty. Lost at sea. Mother cleans the salt shaker like crystal. She cleans the crystal. Wipes her tears. The question in Trivial Pursuit where the answer was 'a bottle.' The answer was 'buried in the garden.' The answer was 'a pool of tears.' And God I saw a phantom. Cats in terracotta planters, dolls in crocheted sweaters, hamsters spinning in wheels. Hurricane Gloria tore out the lilacs with her fingers, snapped my bra strap. She was a phantom, a direct descendent. I spent Christmas upstairs, painting candy cane stripes on my nails.

Pachyderm

She liked the sad circus songs, love songs, songs about babies and their mothers, enormous with memory, reaching their trunks through the bars of their cages. When she heard them, her fingers ached at the tips. They did what they were trained to do. Folded in her folding chair, pretending there wasn't an elephant in the room.

It's called a trunk and you heave it. You pack it full and you reach with it. You load it with books and bags and school pictures and you slam it shut. How tight does your skin sit? How leathered is your memory? There is a name for when fingers get trained to open lockers, yours and your best friend's and your boyfriend's locker. And when it locks it locks. There's a name for when your body misses limbs that went away.

There's a name for the bars and the chains, for tassels and podiums, for crowds and for trumpets, a name for what we're born with and what we learn. And everyone says, look at the baby elephant! Look at the sad, gray balloon. What's a pyramid but the girl on top? What are you without your boyfriend? What's an elephant without its sagging trunk? What's your locker combination, without your memory?

Chick Flicks

She says *passion for fashion* so many times fast 'til the entire mall only confuses me. 'Til the food court is just another place to eat pizza slices and Cinnabons split down the middle, place to cultivate fever. She says she hates girls, says she's not really a girl and I'm supposed to believe her. 'Cause girls believe each other.

In my room, I've been focusing on the windowsill, on the fact that I have a Kewpie doll and a bottle of rosebud nail polish that stand at the exact same height. She says, *How tall are you?* Focus. On the TV there's a girl saying she could never be bulimic. She hates throwing up. Loves food too much. Focus. Saying, *It's thirty degrees outside hun. Put some clothes on.* I'm worried about the fit of my new sweater and how many layers I'll need in this weather.

It's not fair how her name comes up everywhere. On all the keychains in grocery stores and the movies about girls walking around the suburbs. We squealed at the glow-in-the-dark silver guppy fish-facing its way through the Chinese restaurant aquarium. We screeched at books filled with pictures of dogs in sweaters. There was a puffy vanilla show dog and a sad squishy brown dog; one small and one smaller and best friends forever and we squeezed hands and stomped feet and fake-swooned on the sidewalk. And the world cracked down the middle.

We laid down on the couch with a bowl of popcorn, cotton swabs and Kleenex. If I could just last in this body 'til the end of *Beache*s. 'Til the pretty girl says, *I was so jealous of you I could barely see straight.* And then she dies. She gets on the phone while the tape rewinds.

I know exactly what her mother must have felt like, calling her in again and again for dinner. Her calls drowning in the sounds of all the girls screaming outside, *We won, we won! We won, we won, we won!*

Ivy, The Name of this Poem is Secret

Everyone says this book will change your life. But Ivy says her life never changes. She calls up everyone she knows and says, *Tag. You're it*. There's all this talk about an old woman who lives in a shoe with too many children to know what to do and an old man who holds the whole world in his hands like a bowling ball. Hysteria. And he rolls it.

Ivy says you know there are sometimes little mossy rivers, in woods behind houses where you'd never think to find them. She thought she saw him, coming at her in the crosswalk, swinging his arms and grinning past the countdown and she thought, this is it. This is now. This is finally happening. I drilled my whole head out and you're finally here. Sometimes in the woods there are real secret gardens. Sometimes the trees splinter and you have to take a deep, long look at your hands.

Can you see him? We used to look for hidden pictures in magazines. And we'd scribble in notebooks, hide our own names. It's hardest to find a name when it stretches the entire length and width of the page. She went to the back of the gold leaf dictionary, quizzed me on all the presidents. She told me all the secrets hidden in the green of a dollar bill. Ivy's answering machine says there's green poison somewhere deep in the castle. And you know it. Leave a message after the beep.

For Cera

My enormous leopard print saltwater pearl brooch requires a lot of support. Don't you want to look at it and say something fucking stupid like, is that thing gonna squirt water at me or what? Is there a hidden camera in there? This poem is half tribute to the girl dinosaur in *The Land Before Time* and half unrelenting memory. What's that there on your sweater?

I've hired a choir of beautiful teenaged girls to tell our story, Cera, I turned our toothbrushes so that the bristles were touching. And you still wouldn't listen. You'd barely even look at me.

Some cities are prone to earthquakes and other cities are prone to the everyday. We both know that sex is inextricably tied to love. The quotidian. The grocer's freezer. There's igneous and there's sedimentary and there's me throwing pebbles at your window.

And I Will Always Love You

Three stories above the field and
pine trees circling blacktop
in the corner of the school cafeteria
if two people stand next to each other   holding hands
each one facing one of two adjacent juice machines
and if each touches their index finger to the
keyhole of their juice machine
will a shock shoot through both bodies?
Could you do it with anyone
wherever you are
I urge you to find the juice machines/ are they
everywhere or only in one particular school where
some two children thought to hold hands
to make a chain between two keyholes, and every
first day of school, the shop teacher told a story
of a boy who locked himself in the closet, sat down
crushed every bone in his foot with a hammer/ this was
an example of what not to do
with your body/   with the machinery/
how many of us heard
the shriek of the table saw   plank of wood
    bound in the bar clamp
constant beat of your pulse   finger pressed into artery
outside by the white spray-painted finish line
all the cheering/ the surrounding
pushing you/ can do it, come on, you can do it.

Valentine's Day

When Andi said don't I have a beautiful body
and clutched the skeleton key.

I saw two sorority sisters today
and they were wearing brown sorority sweaters
with gold sorority letters. On the contrary,
I don't want distance at all. Not at all.
If you're ever bored up in the attic,
you can rearrange the letters in my name.
If you ever need a recommendation, just light another candle.
One of the sorority girls had long red hair
and feathered bangs, a great figure, California weather,
a show of hands if you were wrong all along.

The drinking fountain in the park squirted water
so cold it could only mean one thing, if you
know what I mean, and I know that you don't.
Cold water nipped my lip and now I have the blues.
Alyssa has a handful of violets.
Alyssa has a lavender lunch pail and a matching headband.
When the roll is called, she always says, *Present.*

The megaphone is a black hole. Forgive me.
The plumbing system under the drinking fountain
leads deep into the ground and lets out into the attic.
Every day is Valentine's Day in the attic.
Every day is a varsity letter sewn into her jacket.
This is all hearsay—heard it with my ear to the ground.
Heard it from the *I* at the end of her name.
Every freckle on her body is an auburn heart; I just know.
Every spider in the attic is building a sweater; I just do.
I'm in the fabric. I can't find my way out of the fabric.
Every thread is a live wire. Every letter is a love letter.

The Cute Beatle

Every single groove in the record paved a path to your house.
Music notes folded in halves and quarters
swirling down where the marigolds grow.

How do marigolds grow? Red shells spill all over the garden
and the multiplication tables keep multiplying.

To be one millionth of a mania, Liverpool,
a puddle that pleads like a vital organ,
picture frame on the bedside table,
entire calendar of months to live for.

Counting the spots on my back,
one piece of a story,
one fourth of an infestation.

The speaker pounded, *Please don't go*,
so I stayed. Daisies on a plastic razor.
I heard baby blocks tinkering above my head,
blue music the entire time I knew you.

One chamber of a heart,
back of a Volkswagen, light
somewhere in or outside of the tunnel.

For Cera

He mumbled something about being ideologically opposed to keeping animals as pets. I always found myself lying next to him chanting, *nature, nature, nature.* I wear the food chain double-looped around my neck.

Cera, Cera. What is a triangle? One charm on the necklace looks like a key. I keep wanting to say that he was so tall and I was so short and our hair was the exact same color as the darkest leopard spots, pinned deep into my sweater, as if something really remarkable had happened. You fought a Sharptooth once, Cera, so you say. Something really remarkable had happened. The earth shook and cracked down the middle, hot salt water. Some people cry; some people fight. The height difference and my pearl brooch was really remarkable. Some boys eat plants some girls eat meat some dinosaurs have three horns.

California

We carved out the lid and scraped pumpkin guts for fall. Megan was a container. Where she's from, people eat oranges all the time and their skin shines. She sits exactly still, watching the travel channel. She said I'm gonna teach you how to draw and then I knew how to draw. She turned me into an old lady by following the wrinkles in my face, painting them deep laundry shades of gray and brown, and we wore old lady hats with violets on them and went to the dog bakery. We took pictures in the summer at the million rose garden where people carve their names in benches and then get married. All the flowers pulled their petals together, self-contained, posed, at home.

She was a girl who hung kites in her room, had a bearded dragon with a hot rock. She couldn't walk in the hallways at our high school 'cause they were too crowded, 'cause her body was too electrically charged and blue bolts shot out of her fingers. Sometimes she saw nice girly ghosts caught in the corners of the ceiling while she was traveling, had a proclivity for hotel fires and wore three washers from her boyfriend's skateboard as rings on her fingers. We fell asleep on a plane talking about gypsies in Italy. When we woke up all her rings were gone. Megan,

I've been using geography as an excuse for everything. One time we were going sixty in a twenty-five, wearing fake eyelashes for the carnival and she said this place. Makes me crazy. How the cars move down the street and the people move in hallways like they're cars. They say the whole world is. Falling apart, but it isn't. They say crow's-feet and listen past the trees for thunder clapping. They count the seconds in the sky and say everything. Is so far away.

And her car's interior was soft leather and vanilla. And we carved the pumpkin into a shark with jagged teeth and fins. We baked the seeds and ate them watching TV with the lizard in our laps. He eats live crickets, crunches them whole. His skin gets dark when he's sad. When he's cold, his entire body flattens.

What Happened in the Pool

I could open my eyes under water, a formation of girls like a flower, lips petal pink. Loves me, loves me not, will never forget me, dives like a Neapolitan ice cream cup. Ashley the Acrobat, Tracy the Tongue Depressor, Candice the Carnival Apple. Tell me there's no *I* in team. There's no hole in the ozone, no scream in ice cream. I could see everything through your bathing suit, everything. Guilt as solitary, a kickboard, a mishap, a sky. I laid my body on top of the water, *floating*. The sky is made of Lycra. Chocolate-syrup solar eclipse, maraschino cherry, hole in the ozone. I could touch the bottom. I could lick the spoon.

The Haunted House

1.
Dear Libby, You can't be friends with a phantom.
They never call you. They never even have a phone.

2.
The way his lazy limp wrist shook the juice bottle oh.

3.
No matter how much I rearrange my furniture,
there are only so many places it can go.

4.
To say I love you is to commit an act of violence.

5.
The wind is blowing in the garden path
between the Emily Dickinson house
and your old house.

6.
Libby's flannel pajamas are covered with spotted dogs,
gray dog bones, and bubbles exclaiming, *Fetch! Speak! Stay!*

7.
I like my body. I like my body.

8.
He told me I shouldn't shave my legs.
Don't do what the patriarchy wants you to do.

9.
Monogamy is a function of capitalism
and love its subsequent product.
An emotional connection is an economic interaction,
as in, a property exchange.

10.
Dear Libby, There's months and months of getting ready,
and then there's the prom. And then there's the post-prom.

11.
There is no guillotine in this building.

12.
I can't look at your house without wanting to collapse it.
I can't close my eyes without seeing glow-in-the-dark
    shrieking skulls.

13.
His hand was pressed into my back.
There was a merry-go-round at the end of the movie.

14.
Dear Libby, It looks like you're writing a letter.
It looks like you're watching TV.

15.
When I woke up, I asked him if I was acting crazy in my sleep.
He said no, just that in my sleep I kept opening
 my eyes and asking if I was acting crazy.

16.
A riddle: What bleeds every month but does not die?

17.
When you press her button, Barbie says, *Math class is tough!* Press it again and she says, *I think it's something too complicated to be simplified in a way that makes it possible to explain it in terms of how what I want is probably rooted in ideologies that are fueled by capitalism and therefore somehow violent and reactionary and somewhat problematic in some respects.* Press it again and she says, *Let's plan our dream wedding!*

18.
A riddle: What's weightless, can be seen by the naked eye,
and when you put it into a barrel, it will make the barrel lighter?

19.
There was so much excitement in the way he kept slamming his alarm clock all morning.

20.
Libby couldn't decide who she bought the dancing skeleton for.
And one by one everybody's birthday passed by.

21.
To save this message forever and ever and ever and ever and ever, press 9.

22.
I had a dream that Madonna and I were attempting to move an enormous piece of lawn furniture down an extremely narrow wooden staircase in the rain. She was playing a benefit concert in my hometown, and I told her that everyone was elated, that the other performers were all really popular but that she is an immensely important musical icon. She said that her favorite Madonna song was "Get Into the Groove." I told her that mine was too.

23.
Dear Libby, I keep forgetting to tell you about the man who plays your goodnight song in the train station, your song about little boys in boats, crossing freezing cold rivers.

24.
We knew the diamond was real because it scratched the glass window.

25.
And I walked home in the dark, in the snow. I shouldn't have gone.
Libby, when you grow up, just don't even go.

26.
A riddle: What did one ghost say to the other?

27.
The part of the song when she says,
At night I lock the doors/ where no one else can see.

28.
Dear Libby, Do not open the door if you're not prepared to close it.
The demons will keep on piling in. They will come and go as they please.

29.
On Libby's favorite show, the bad guy has a shrinking machine. It makes millions of little people that are just like him, only smaller.

30.
The night the glitter from my new shirt got all over his sheets and stuck to his skin,

31.
The carnival ride where the boy's supposed to sit on the inside and the girl's supposed to sit on the outside, so when the spinning starts she slides into him. I thought we were being radical when we switched seats. I thought we were being radical but really you were just crushing me.

32.
The desire to be touched is an act of oppression.

33.
We covered the hole in the kitchen wall with Libby's kindergarten paintings.

34.
I had a dream I bashed his face in with a baseball bat,
a dream the paint stripped off the walls in paper-thin shrieks.

35.
It was like the episode of *90210* when Brenda and Dylan can't
    stop making out in public.
It was like the episode of *Family Ties* when Jennifer leaves her
    own birthday party with the popular girls.

36.
Dear Libby, The Ghost Ship swings left and right and sometimes keeps going in a complete circle.

37.
I can't stop wanting to curl your daguerreotype's hair
    and give her a ruffled collar —

38.
Intercourse is an act of possession in which a man inhabits a woman, over her and inside her. This physical relation, this male possession, becomes an affirmation.

39.
I want a diamond on my finger.
I want a diamond the size of a house on my finger.

40.
Dear Libby, I'll never forget that summer when yellow jackets spilled in through the attic fan. He gave me a rubber stamp that said, *Keep in Touch,* with a little bear wearing a bow in her hair. You kept turning all the soda in the house into those stupid little ice cube popsicles.

41.
They said the Titanic was a ship that could never sink.
They say you can't talk to a man with a shotgun.

42.
Saturday night I stumbled proudly down a spiral staircase
and walked face-first into a glass door.

43.
If there's a future, all the robots will have rectangular metal hands.

44.
We were listening to the Stevie Nicks record where her hair is flying like a wild coyote, and she's holding a tambourine in her hand like a mirror for the whole entire world to look into.

45.
Dear Libby, Call me tomorrow or I'll call you.

46.
The disconnect of who he was from what he would do
like how when someone dies, they divide into two
and one floats up to the ceiling.

47.
The words *Called back*, her last written message, are the
words that now appear on Emily Dickinson's tombstone.

48.
Libby has her very own phone line.
Libby has a neon pink fluorescent glowing phone.

49.
The weird fantasy I have that he pulls me away somewhere at
    a party,
starts kissing me, and "Fast Car" by Tracy Chapman is playing.

50.
A riddle: You want to go home, but the man in the mask is there.

51.
It was like the episode where Brenda falls asleep on the beach, wakes up with an awful sunburn.

52.
I could have sworn that Anne Frank referred to herself as a gusher in her diary, but she didn't. And then I thought it must have been Katherine in Judy Blume's *Forever*, but no.

53.
Dear Libby, I can still see you,
making one of those bridges with your body
by bending over backward.

54.
He was reading Woody Allen out loud and I was laughing,
wearing enormous Jackie O sunglasses as we waited for the light
    to change.

55.
A man walking around the lake with a baby looked at me and said,
See that? That's a park bench. That is a park bench.

56.
Theoretically speaking, Katherine should have been happy being alone at the end of *Forever*. But she wasn't.

57.
Libby's afraid of the dark,
big bad wolves on the walls every time she blinks.

58.
Some women marry houses.
It's another kind of skin.

59.
Something about Emily Dickinson's grave, or her letter, something about how the ground was *calling* me.

60.
Libby has a collection of sequins that she found stuck to her ballet shoes.

61.
Dear Libby, This swan dive is for you.

Tidal

Nature is a Haunted House —
but Art — a House that tries to be Haunted.

—Emily Dickinson

it's exhausting
being everybody all the time
exhausting   [vulgar]
giggling under water

stamping a tiny feminine foot
at God   a tantrum

history   running
through Emily Dickinson's legs
leap frog

history   to see it lap the Miles

if beauty is a dead girl
                a garden
would you lift up her skirt

she who unhooked the lane lines,
did a mermaid dive

shaking a giant Promethean fist
                punching bag

airtight in that   corset
lungs expanding

and what if when she finally spoke
she wouldn't ever   shut up.

Indian Summer

It was so hot the way you helped me transition into high school. Baseball diamonds rocked themselves to sleep at night. The way the air is so perfect and crisp at Halloween-time and the streets get dark so early. There's a moth in the house, eyes all over its wings. I sleep with the covers over my head. You threw a penny into the fish pond and it landed in my mouth. Libby said, *Native Americans, Mom.* The ghost-quiet girl voice at the end of the song. The way my grandma bounced a ball off the front stoop in the 30s, ate penny candy. Scrawled in my diary, *My life is a great depression.* I put my tongue in your mouth, as a joke. The way she told us not to cry over spilled milk, literally. When I was wasted in the top bunk, laughing, pulled a foot-long string of goo out of my eye. How it's kind of like an entire town underneath the Christmas tree, if you think about it. True love your mother's head in your father's lap, crying. When you call me, if you call me, I'll say, *I was just thinking about you.* And you'll say, *Oh yeah, what were you thinking?*

Swimming in Lanes Five and Six

Emily Dickinson chipped my tooth with her head while I was breathing under my left arm and she was sloppily coming out of her flip-turn. I found forty bound fascicles of poems in her locker. She told me the combination once. She told me to use leave-in conditioner.

They said Emily resembled a large white moth in a red swimming cap, practicing her butterfly. She drove a hearse, almost. We were scared to death. And I miss her, the way we banged on the lockers and cheered before swim meets, how she would write poems and fold them into love notes, propel off the diving block.

She rammed her head into my mouth, in the pool. I hid her letters in my bra. There's a part of my brain that's like the zipper on a sleeping bag, a cluster of pine trees, a telephone cord. Like Emily Dickinson, if she spent all her time after school in the pool and her clothes were always getting doused with water. And she sat behind me in class with wet hair, tapping her fingers on the desk, humming.

Swan Song

She was so red/ so red/ veterinarian. Dear Red, I want to paint your room. Unabashedly gift-wrapped, two red birds with little military plumes.

There's no such thing as the telephone. I came in an ambulance. I fell from a tree. My baby bird, a process of gaining weight slowly, losing it again/ maybe we could invent a telephone.

Her little foot scraped on the pavement. Her little leg snapped like a twig. Tug the yarn between our two windows. Take this wafer/ styrofoam/ it's a secret.

My mouth picks up the radio and it's playing our song. Crickets chirping 4ever. My mouth tastes like conversation, tissue paper the color of the walls in your room.

I drilled out the bottom of a paper cup/ body buried in the garden. Two red birds in a shoe box/ I cut the yarn in the middle. I curled the ends of red ribbon with the scissors.

Under the Evergreens

You were talking to me about the prominent role that female friendship played in Emily Dickinson's poems, but it was in a message on my answering machine and while I was listening I accidentally deleted the message. And this is a prequel.

You called me up and started talking in a fake voice about Emily Dickinson's life and her poetry, militant visions for mutual reciprocity/ *he kissed me*. How she sent valentines from the top of the stairs. I knew it was you the whole time/ didn't/ called you back and the phone just kept on ringing and ringing I guess because you weren't home.

I called your cell phone but it went straight to voicemail and your outgoing message said things can't be the way they were when we were younger, that the attic is filling up with water and damned if you are going to lay down and die like that.

You read into the phone the Emily Dickinson poem that's like "Walk on the Ocean" by Toad the Wet Sprocket. Like the hollow feeling after the sleepover/ *impossible*. We'd put on mascara and listen to music to try to make ourselves cry.

It was April Fool's Day when he asked me to marry. I called you up to tell you and you said that Emily Dickinson's poetry approaches the theme of marriage in a complex and elliptical and radical manner, and then static. I meant to seal the envelope and send the letter. I meant to clutch the poison but instead I swallowed the ring.

A Letter

- In the font of *My Clip-on Earrings Are Killing Me.*
  (not) *My Clip-on Earrings Killed Me:*

I'm so hungry I could eat a horse. Nine Venus Flytraps sweating on the back porch. And I call you Aphrodite, my mood ring says I'm dying. I'm so hungry I could eat myself for lunch.

- In the font of *please, please, please:*

I was falling asleep on the bus thinking about the concentric circles of "Hey Joe," wherein nothing actually happens.

- In the font of *Madwoman in the Attic:*

I was a cutter. Your body was peach fuzz-covered. The music was blaring in the blue room and we didn't know what on earth to do with our eyes.

- In the font of *Have You Heard Oh My God of Breasts Like Moons:*

You know exactly who you are. You know exactly what you do.

- In the font of *I Came Here Tonight to Find My Friends:*

I open my mouth and say *ah* to every click in the slideshow. How she slid through the window, snapped the lid on her poison ring and followed the spider out.

- In the font of *Tonsil Hockey and Pretend Prostitution:*

Holler at me from outer space. My ponytail is gathering dust.

- In the font of *Kick Me in the Shins Written on the Mirror in Lipstick:*

I wanted to tell you about Moon River. How I went to the hairdresser with a pile of eyes torn out from fashion magazines, said, *Here, do this to me.*

- In the font of *Pink Lemonade:*

They say to make lemonade, to creep your hands along the walls of the house. Before she was a ghost, she was a girl like me, her brother playing on the computer all night. Dear Emilie, I mean marmalade, I mean, lemonade. All my clothes were bubblegum pink and all of his were lemon yellow.

This Summer

If you want to spin the bottle to anywhere, fake-faint at parties I will be there. All the insects swarm around in your stomach. Angie, at the mall, eye shadow, etcetera, your pink walls cradle the girl baby. Toy train swarms around the attic. The steam pours out in hearts, exhaust. *The Swoon God sends us Women.* It's simple: the yellow jacket impulse to kill, the caterpillar turning slow in rings of smoke, the butterfly. Above the pool, little wings flap like the shutter on Angie's camera. Look directly into the hole in the center of the hive. Angie's eyelashes look alive. She burned her fingertip on a firefly. You can't fall in love when you're out pollinating. You can lie completely still but it won't stop the train from moving. Dear Angie, somewhere something entirely pure. Go to parties. Get boys. Don't fall backward too hard but be there, your hair still stings me, such a dramatic swoop.

For Cera

Who was the dominant herbivore? Do you want to play fetch? I want to link and unlink your jewelry. I want you to pinch me when you're pinching a pill off my sweater.

There was a red-hot lava river flowing down the fissure between bed and wall, hard to see through all the steam. And a great many of the rocks we kick outside are made of hardened lava/ yeah right, and I'm the bad guy. And Cera I'm so sorry. And the very earth that we walk on was once inhabited by giant reptilian monsters.

Yellow jackets

The bees were crowding up a fluorescent ceiling light and overflowing. They welted my arms purple in my dream where I couldn't run. Did you scream? Did you leap into lakes? Was it magic? Were there branches? Did you make it? Did someone kiss you? I thought, no, my bee-sting dreams are not important. But they're mine. They happen to me.

Why do they come in the windows? What exactly are they looking for? I know that they also make honey, help flowers, and we should know enough to relax, to trust nature to work in this way.

Do you know me? I can't move when I see them and the entire world rushes at me from the window. There are two directions to choose from: over and under. There are trees and there is also water. Were you alone? Baby? Did it hurt? Did you scream? Sometimes I think that I could never have children, for the bees. That there are two directions to go. That children like to play outside and they also like sugar, etcetera. I have seen yellow jackets crowding the lemonade pitcher and spilled plastic cups and it was enough for me that I did not scream. We could have children, even though we are petrified of bees, even though there are bees that will kill us and our children and even though I have sacrificed other people's children to syrup-drunk yellow bees and might do the same with my own. And even though you want all stacks of books, no room for children, for fever and band-aids and pillows and blankets. Is there a button? A lever? A way to know? There are two directions we can go.

There was a wasp in your room once, and I looked at you. And you looked back at me and said, *I don't know what to do.* You said, *What should I do?* Do you know me? I know all about you. There are two directions we can go. Did you scream? Did you fall to a sheet? Did you make it? People live with one another in houses with medicine cabinets, and they call each other *honey*, and one runs screaming with the children if there are children and there should be children, and the other walks to the window and calmly kills the bee.

From the Place Where All the Postcards Come

I had to touch fingertips, bring you to the movie theater where I got my first kiss and push you through the eyelets in the radiator. I had to teach you sleeping bags like learning to spell, to let you break your arm so I could sign your cast. Say *keep me*, say *goldfish color*. I had to tell you they were pennies in the pool and they were. They would have been if they hadn't kept getting bigger.

I had to take you to the outside shower near the willow and practice saying the weight the sand would take, saying my hair like seaweed and telling me it's jellyfish season. Tell me all your cousins' names and stop crying. Spell their names in circles and get lost in the rhythm.

I had to find you in a wicker swing, sing you a song about babies in baskets. I sleep in a tent outside where girls play cards hard 'til they're fighting. I gather hot pink newts and store them in sand. I wish you were. I shake the chalk castle 'til the sand shocks.

A baby bird told me the sidewalk was hot enough to fry an egg. That you were as black and white as the newspapers said you'd be. When your arms made an O it was just a hole, just a hook to throw in lakes when your fingers made a J. She went in the backyard to fight with the girls. And the sun broke yolk. And you're not. And the baby bird was right, stomped her feet on pavement. The showerhead beat down because it had to.

I Drew a Door

All anyone ever wanted to talk about was Tricia's extra vagina, how does it feel and what does it look like and how does it work and how big is it, how she could technically be pregnant twice at the same time. To dip their hands in it like a museum exhibit. One says, *Surprise!* The other says, *It's for you.*

Tricia drew me a diagram of her two vaginas on a beer-splotched napkin in Hooters. She drew a very narrow canal and a trapdoor and all the leakage, all the leakage, straight hard pencil shots. At work she'd push the steamer up and down the creases of skirts and dresses, remember him when she saw the little bruises on her arms.

And one vagina is very small and the other one is bigger. One vagina is social; the life of the party, and the other is shy and introverted, modest and artistic. One is at the mall and the other's at the library. One stays and one scatters. One says, *I'm sorry*, puts a hand in her hair, says *Hey, I'm really sorry.* One says, *I forgive you.*

For Cera

Cera, Cera, no time is a good time/ Cera,
our communications are getting so meta,
so mangled. I keep getting your songs
stuck in my head. I keep finding myself
looking for you in the mirror. There
is a hidden camera where I can still go
watch you swimming around in the water.
I move my fingertips in little soft circles
on my skull. You keep saying my eyelashes
are so long, pressing into my temples.
Cera, mascara wand and the ravine
was so high, so you say. Your frills are
made of bone and we were born this way.

Water

If a tree falls in the forest, does she make a sound? Can you/ could you even hear me? What's Helen Keller's favorite color? Can you receive text messages on this phone? I want to be in the finished basement/ can you feel the fever? I want to be part of the finished basement. We were all in the car driving around in the lines of your black and white plaid overalls. What's black and white and/ I know how to float in the ocean. There must be a way to work this VCR. All I need is a miracle, whatever, Helen Keller and the Helen Keller coloring book. If I were a wall/ tell her to find the corners in a round room. If I were a wall in the finished basement you'd look at me and say, *I feel like I'm talking to a wall*. I killed a mosquito with that book. Why does the mosquito hum into our ears at night/ tell me the story. If I were in the finished basement/ tell me again. You looked just like George Washington when you flipped your hair over your head in the pool. There were bubbles flying out of your lips. So I couldn't read them, water made it hard to hear/ the part of the Helen Keller movie when the entire family used to stand up and cheer.

Me Without Makeup

In the kitchen, there are various sets of graduated hanging baskets. On the street, all the claw machines play the exact same carnival song. Take a left after the first claw machine. If you reach the second claw machine, you've gone too far.

A boy on the basketball court is wearing a reversible t-shirt with removable felt letters. I'm wearing the same t-shirt in reverse, with the letters rearranged. I look at him and he gives me the *Wonder Years* wave. When I turn on my phone, it exclaims, *Welcome!* And balloons soar and confetti pops and fireworks burst in the air. Are you there, God? It's me. Did you know it was me? You didn't, did you. The magnetic poetry on the refrigerator spells out a *your mom* joke. It takes everything in me just to screw in the light bulb.

A perfect blue wave crashes into the shore on a Starbucks sugar packet on the counter. I knew it was you because I saw up my own skirt in the mirror clipped onto your shoe. We stayed up all night to see the end of the Freddy Krueger movie. We spent all winter watching reruns of shows set in previous decades. We drove around listening to the "Wind of Change" by the Scorpions, on repeat.

Book Eater

I watched all the Winona Ryder movies

but I only wished I was watching you.

There's a worm in my apple

glowing green-apple green.

I tried to squeeze the movie like a sponge.

Cut the book to its core. Catch the worm.

Dear worm, Dear eye,

Deer fly, fruit fly,

My ears are ringing, so I know you're still around.

My ears are buzzing.

The worm slides inside and outside of the apple.

Yum Poison Apple

The death of a beautiful woman is unquestionably the most poetical topic in the world
—Edgar Allan Poe

I'm not a woman; I'm a force of nature.
—Courtney Love

Death is not objective. Grunge is not hereditary. Beauty is neither a range of controls nor a series of ambiguities, body shapes/ I wanted.

I found Kurt's ocean wave pinky ring underneath my radiator, *treasure*. Secrets spilled out of the Ouija board/ Ouch. I wanted. I spent all morning getting the *I slept in my makeup* look. *Seventeen* says masturbation teaches the difference between sex and love.

It's an anti-rape song/ never forget. I listen to it three times before the school bus comes so I can have it in my head all day/ and blood-red lipstick, barely-there lipstick, deep-seated sentimentality, *the comfort in being sad.*

Beauty is inherent in the lyric. Grunge is a big mess/ raw sound. The cooler the voice, the warmer the reception. *Someday you will ache like I ache.*

Jenny's got a perfume bottle that's shaped like a woman's body. Stop moving. Like that time I died on the playground and you woke me up/ A slug fell asleep on my arm, burned its shape there. Poison apple. A songbird's soothing. I flew off the swing set, went up, up,

For Cera

Cera, is my mascara running, my dish
water splashing, I can see the blue paint
leaking onto your green scales.

Blink. Is your frill like a bridal veil?
I'll say I think it looks cool, click
over. Your eyelashes make you
look like a girl. Does your home
feel empty, does your ring finger throb,
does the bridge reach across the ravine?

I sign my letters *xo*,
hunter green. Cera.
My barrel's all you at the bottom.
My squirt gun has your eyelashes.
Detergent bubbles on the dishes. Blink.

Skull & Crossbones

I sucked in freezing cold air like it was cherry cola, just anticipating you. My Virgin Mary, diary key, if you would let me. Subzero weather under the covers. You. In the font of *there is still hope under the ground*. I dyed my hair Cola, split the penny roll open. It was a blessing from God in Heaven, the copper pennies, wishing well, holy water, rain and my unwashed hands and all.

In the font of *when it rains it rains*. Dear Diary, I dyed my hair Passion Plum. Icebox Plum. In the font of *they were so sweet and so cold*. The inherent instability of social relationships like a bottle of poison under the sink. Your hair was outrageous, pointed me in every direction. It was in the bible, descending like a swan dive. It was in the *Guinness Book of World Records*.

The Logician

She wanted her hair braided, wanted it pulled hard. She wanted a grandmother to remember, an ancestral tie like a rainbow shoelace, roots carved deep as a stomp-stomp in the cellar.

They taught her to make two bows. They told her to see them as two bunny ears and that this rabbit was more or less a child as she was a child and that rabbits sometimes steal from gardens when they are hungry or when they are mischievous and that if the rabbit over which she squealed and shrieked in the neighbor's garden was more or less a child, then she is a child but is also more or less that rabbit's mother.

She was her mother's daughter. Her mother was her grandmother's daughter. Sometimes people's fathers shoot rabbits and eat them when they are hungry and sometimes a child that is a child as she is a child is hungry but cannot eat and instead will cry, will dribble tears for days and weeks until their bones show.

She was shown a message preceding a commercial that this commercial was not intended for a sensitive audience and she was told repeatedly that this message meant that she should run from the room where she sat on the arm of her grandmother's couch, running a powder-pink comb through her grandmother's toy poodle hair.

Briar Rose

How the carnations suck up all the green food coloring/ your eyes.
How the blue rose glows, swizzle stick, blossoms in a dark room.

I took pictures for you of the aurora borealis. We lost touch.
The glass that rolls up on the beach, smooth and green, the girl.
I always imagined that Sleeping Beauty was sleeping in a coffin/

Girl pricks finger/ Green River
grows like a rose
like that time I was born/
grows like a gnarled hedge of thorns
like that time I died/
that time I woke up/

I found pieces of pink light in the grit under your fingernails,
yellow cake. I'm awake and you're asleep. I shook the book.
    Wake up!
I shook the river. Emerald green water, soaking wet leaves.
I flip through the story, kiss the last page.

Riding in Cars with Monsters

I got hit with the ugly stick, and stuff. Woke up in a pool of monster sweat. The monster finds love so easily. The monster finds real love everywhere. Under rocks and buried in sand, behind trees, tangled in seaweed, love, love, love. The monster has
a) enormous hearts for eyes
b) a locket with my picture in it
c) a fever

I got my father's sense of humor, caught all the jokes as they poured down the slide. The slippery/slope/of/reproductive/technology, etcetera, etcetera, etcetera, and I still hear the monster moaning.

I'll create steps for the monster. I'll create stairs. A pond with skipping stones. Monstrous how the CD skips at my favorite part in the song. I know you, I listen and I hear your claws, paws, fangs. If this is music, it's got a scar running down its middle. If this is music, it's got pull like a black hole.

The monster stole all my pajamas. If I could I would. The monster slammed on the brakes. Or I did, either way. I cracked open my fortune cookie. I walked outside. There was some kind of natural phenomenon happening in the sky.

Called Back

Every time I called you, you picked up the phone. Your tight wire curls like cords. Hi, who is it? I put oil on the tips of my hair, shadow on my eyelids. You always picked up the phone, always painted straight from a picture, or, all your paintings were real people. And that's what I loved about you: simplicity. Like, every girl needs a good little black dress.

You said I had "Bette Davis eyes," which I later learned also means "sad eyes." You said that I had "Bette Davis eyes," which is something that makes it easy to picture my face on your pillow. To picture my eyes in particular, miniature blue throws. *She knows just what it takes to make a girl blush* and *All the boys think she's a spy.* The binary is awkward and unbalanced and explosive. Which also means, a perfect song for dancing.

Every time I called you, you picked up the phone. Pictured me on top of you, thinking about you. Pictured me hiding under blankets. The connection: say it's a trap door, a keyhole, a camera. *Her hands are never cold.* Say we were dancing and the lights cut out. Say he slid his hands in through the holes in the phone and that's all I remember.

I Had Never Felt So Much Like a Cake Made up of a Variety of Ingredients

Hold up your lighter and light my candles. The icing is a layer. She was my mother. She was my favorite cousin. She was wrong; a liar; we all were. There's a part in the movie where the heart is a heart-shaped cookie. A photograph deep in a shoebox deep in my closet, broken glass where the heart is a shape formed by chocolate chip cookies. The cake in the window says, *God Bless You, Amy.* Save your childhood. A gingerbread house inside your house. If I want to borrow something. If I want to be your mail-order bride. If I want to back away from you slowly. The arch of your back, stirring the fire like your grandfather stirred bathtub gin. I have my grandmother's earrings. The ruffles of her dress: gone. Hair: brown. Your eyes: enormous, gumdrop green.

Artifacts

The creak in the door got stuck in my spinal cord.

The creak in the floor board/

You pulled up the covers.   My eyelids are
    green, white, moving.

You said mixing perfumes together makes poison/

I used to believe you.   Wished on a wishbone.

I kept a picture of the forest burning in my locket

a catalogue of candies underneath my pillow.

I value the wood grain. Trace you into the bedpost.

I'm as white as a sheet   I just saw a million ghosts.

NOTES

The Haunted House: Section 17: "Math class is tough" and "Let's plan our dream wedding!" are two of the pre-programmed phrases spoken by Teen Talk Barbie, released by Mattel in 1992. **Section 27:** Lyrics taken from the Madonna song "Get Into the Groove." **Section 38:** Paraphrased from Andrea Dworkin's *Intercourse*. **Section 58:** Taken from Anne Sexton's "Housewife."

Tidal: "To see it lap the Miles" is a line taken from Emily Dickinson's poem #585.

A Letter: *"Madwoman in the Attic"* refers to the book *The Madwoman in the Attic: The Woman Writer and the 19th-century Literary Imagination* by Sandra M. Gilbert and Susan Gubar. "I came here tonight to find my friends" is a lyric taken from the Le Tigre song "Sweetie."

This Summer: "The Swoon God sends us Women" is a line taken from Emily Dickinson's poem #1072.

Yum Poison Apple: "The comfort in being sad" is a song lyric taken from Nirvana's "Frances Farmer Will Have Her Revenge on Seattle." "Someday you will ache like I ache" is taken from the Hole song "Doll Parts."

Skull & Crossbones: Some lines in this poem's second stanza allude to William Carlos Williams' "This Is Just To Say."

Called Back: Italicized words are lyrics taken from the Kim Carnes song "Bette Davis Eyes," though sometimes misquoted.

Author Photo: Barret Gentz.

ABOUT MARISA CRAWFORD

Marisa Crawford grew up in New York and in Connecticut. She graduated from the University of Massachusetts in Amherst, and received her MFA from San Francisco State University. *The Haunted House*, winner of the 2008 Gatewood Prize as selected by Denise Duhamel, is her first book.

ALSO BY SWITCHBACK BOOKS

The Bodyfeel Lexicon
Jessica Bozek

Oneiromance (an epithalamion)
Kathleen Rooney

Our Classical Heritage: A Homing Device
Caroline Noble Whitbeck

Pathogenesis
Peggy Munson

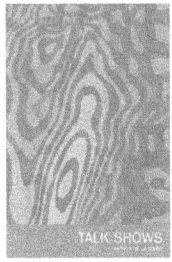

Talk Shows
Mónica de la Torre